TN

EXTREME WEATHER

BLIZZARDS

Liza N. Burby

The Rosen Publishing Group's
PowerKids Press™
New York

Published in 1999 by The Rosen Publishing Group, Inc.
29 East 21st Street, New York, NY 10010

First Edition

Book Design: Resa Listort

Photo Credits: p. 4 © Scott West/The Viesti Collection; pp. 6–7 © Kirk Condyles/Impact Visuals; p. 8 © IBL/The Viesti Collection; p. 11 © Caroline Wood/International Stock; p. 12 © 1997 A.J. Wolfe/Concord Monitor/Impact Visuals; pp. 14–15 © Carlos Villalon/Impact Visuals; p. 16 © Dan Peha/The Viesti Collection; p. 18 © Martha Cooper/Viesti Associates; p. 19 © Corbis-Bettmann; p. 20 © 1985 Wilson North/International Stock.

Burby, Liza N.
    Blizzards / by Liza N. Burby.
        p. cm. — (Extreme weather)
    Includes index.
    Summary: An introduction to the winter storms that cover the earth with snow, including when and where they occur, the damage they can do, how they are predicted, and the dates of some of the worst blizzards in history.
    ISBN 0-8239-5291-6
    1. Blizzards—Juvenile literature. 2. Blizzards—United States—Juvenile literature. [1.Blizzards.]
    I. Title. II. Series.
QC926.37.B87 1998
551.55'5—DC21
            98-15979
              CIP
              AC

Manufactured in the United States of America

Contents

What Is a Blizzard?

Blizzards are storms that cover the earth with blankets of snow. Their **fierce** (FEERS) winds blow snow into deep **drifts** (DRIFTS) and trees and homes get covered with flakes that looks like white frosting. When a blizzard is over, the earth may look like it's sparkling. Both kids and grown-ups can have fun playing in the snow. But blizzards can also be very **dangerous** (DAYN-jer-us). **Meteorologists** (MEET-EE-er-AH-luh-jists) study blizzards to learn more about these strong storms and how people can stay safe during them.

Snow after a storm can be beautiful as it hangs on trees in Yellowstone National Park in Wyoming.

Where and When Do They Happen?

Blizzards usually happen between November and April. Sometimes they occur as early as October or as late as May. Blizzards can occur anywhere, even in places where **temperatures** (TEMP-rah-churz) are usually warm, like in the southern United States. Some of the heaviest blizzards happen in the northern, northwestern, and northeastern parts of the United States. Blizzards begin in the areas around the North and South Poles. This is where the cold air of winter, called **polar** (POH-ler) air, comes from.

The Blizzard of 1994 dumped large amounts of snow on many of New York's Long Island beaches.

How Do Blizzards Start?

Polar air is very cold. When it blows over land during the winter, it's common for a blizzard to get stirred up. Before a blizzard can happen, though, snow has to form. Snow is made when water **vapor** (VAY-per) in the air freezes. This forms ice crystals. Crystals come together around dust **particles** (PAR-tih-kulz) and make clumps. Many clumps will form inside a cloud. When each clump, or group of crystals, gets big enough, it falls from the sky as a snowflake. Many snowflakes falling together are a harmless snowfall. But polar winds added to this snowfall make a dangerous blizzard.

Every snowflake that falls from the sky is different from all other snowflakes.

What Happens During a Blizzard?

Blizzards can last a few hours or a few days. They may stop and then start up again. Blizzard winds can blow up to 35 miles per hour or more. The sound of these winds can be like the roar of a train. The winds push and pull light snowflakes around in all directions. This makes it hard for people to see. A **whiteout** (WYT-owt) is when you can't see because of the blowing, blinding snow.

Whiteouts can be dangerous. It's a good idea to stay indoors if a blizzard becomes a whiteout.

Why Are Blizzards Dangerous?

Whiteouts are dangerous because people can get lost in them, even if they're only a few feet from their own front door. If you are outside in a blizzard for too long, you could get **frostbite** (FROST-byt). But blizzards are bad for other reasons. All the snow can make it hard for cars, trains, and planes to run. People can get **stranded** (STRAN-ded) in their cars during blizzards. Heavy snow can crush a roof or break electric or telephone wires. And when cold temperatures and winds combine, the air feels colder than it actually is. This is called wind chill.

Heavy storms can do a lot of damage and cause extra work for repairworkers.

Different Kinds
of Winter Storms

Not all winter storms are blizzards. A **nor'easter** (nor-EE-ster) is one kind of wild winter storm. They happen in the northeastern part of the United States, and get their name from the strong, northeasterly winds that blow across the Atlantic Ocean. These winds create heavy snow, rain, and very high waves that crash onto beaches and damage houses. They also cause beach **erosion** (ee-ROH-zhun). In the South, ice storms can hit if **moisture** (MOYS-cher) blows over the land when the temperatures are cold enough to freeze that moisture. Then even places that are usually warm are covered with ice.

Many big cities don't have anywhere to dump extra snow after a heavy storm. After the 1996 blizzard in New York City, extra snow was dumped into Manhattan's rivers.

Blizzards Do Strange Things

Blizzards can blow snow into drifts that are as high as a house. Drifts also make strange shapes. A drift that looks like a dinosaur could really be a car covered with snow. Another drift that looks like a giant could really be a tree. Some blizzards have left as much as 51 inches of snow on the ground. That's as tall as a grown-up! All that snow can trap people in their homes. Sometimes blizzard winds pick up old snow that is already on the ground and blow it around as well. When that happens, it's hard to tell whether the snow is coming from the sky or the ground.

Drifts can slide off a roof and bury things on the ground, such as this van.

Blizzards in History

Blizzards are named for the year they happen and where they occur. The worst blizzards in history have shut down entire cities. The Blizzard of 1888 hit the East Coast of the United States from March 10 through 14. In New York City, everyone was taken by surprise. March 9 had been a warm day.

The Blizzard of 1996 shut down all of New York City. New Yorkers who went outside had to walk in the streets—the sidewalks were covered in six-foot snow drifts!

But by March 14, there was over two feet of snow in the city. More than 400 people died in the storm.

The Blizzard of 1888 was another blizzard that stopped New York City in its tracks. New Yorkers of that time had to dig trolley cars and horse-drawn buggies out of the snow.

19

Predicting Blizzards

Most blizzards are known as well-behaved storms. That's because meteorologists can often **predict** (pre-DIKT) when blizzards are coming and how bad they will be. Blizzards usually travel on westerly winds. So if a storm begins in the West, meteorologists know it will head east. They use **radar** (RAY-dar) and a **satellite** (SAT-uh-lyt) to follow a storm. If there is a winter storm watch, that means meteorologists are expecting heavy snow in the next twelve hours. A winter storm warning means that a storm is beginning.

Helicopters are often used to record the amount of damage and snowfall in one area. This photograph was taken from a helicopter.

Safety During a Blizzard

When you hear that a blizzard is coming, remind your parents to check that there are new batteries in your flashlight in case you lose **electricity** (ee-lek-TRIH-sih-tee). Also, make sure there is enough food and water at your house. You may not be able to go outside for several days once a blizzard hits. If you do go outside during the storm, bundle up and try to stay warm. You should wear several layers of clothing and a scarf around your face to protect your skin and lungs from the cold blizzard winds. Blizzards can be beautiful, but it's safer to watch them indoors from the safety and warmth of your home.

Glossary

dangerous (DAYN-jer-us) Able to cause harm.

drift (DRIFT) A pile of snow blown by wind.

electricity (ee-lek-TRIH-sih-tee) A form of energy that produces heat and light.

erosion (ee-ROH-zhun) To be worn away slowly by wind or water.

fierce (FEERS) Very strong and wild.

frostbite (FROST-byt) Damage to the skin when it is exposed to severe cold.

meteorologist (MEET-EE-er-AH-luh-jist) A person who studies the weather.

moisture (MOYS-cher) Water that is in the air.

nor'easter (nor-EE-ster) A strong snowstorm that happens in the eastern part of the United States.

particle (PAR-tih-kul) A small piece of something.

polar (POH-ler) Something near the North or South Poles.

predict (pre-DIKT) To guess about something before it happens.

radar (RAY-dar) A machine that is used to predict a storm's direction.

satellite (SAT-uh-lyt) A machine that is used from space to predict weather.

stranded (STRAN-ded) To be left alone in a scary or hard situation.

temperature (TEMP-rah-chur) How hot or cold something is.

vapor (VAY-per) Tiny water droplets in the air.

whiteout (WYT-owt) When snow from the ground and in the air are blown around, making it hard to see.

Index